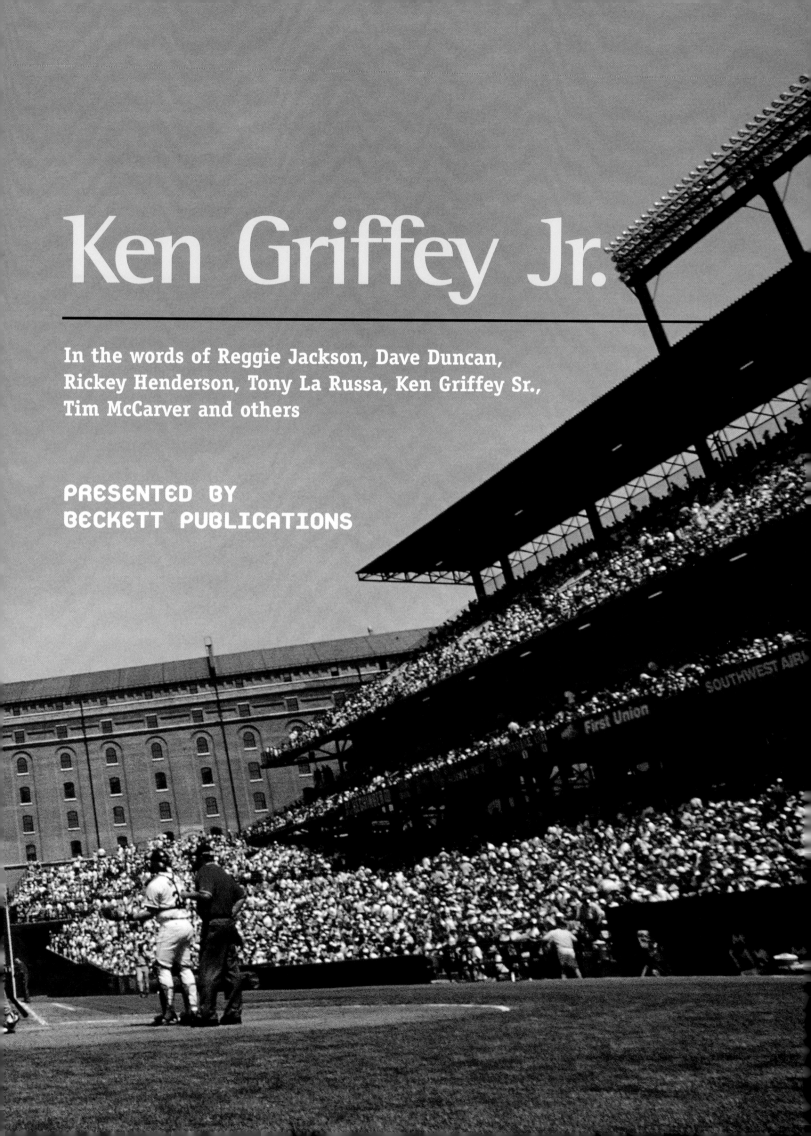

Ken Griffey Jr.

In the words of Reggie Jackson, Dave Duncan,
Rickey Henderson, Tony La Russa, Ken Griffey Sr.,
Tim McCarver and others

PRESENTED BY
BECKETT PUBLICATIONS

Ken Griffey Jr.
In the words of . . .

Published by: Beckett Publications
15850 Dallas Parkway
Dallas, TX 75248

ISBN: 1-887432-64-7

First Edition: March 1999

Beckett Corporate Sales and Information (972) 991-6657

foreword

Ken Griffey Sr.
As told to Claire Smith

On Aug. 31, 1990, I lived the dream that any father would give his right arm to have come true. I stepped onto a major league field with my son, Kenny, as a teammate to play a major league game.

It's still vivid to me. In my first at-bat after my trade from Cincinnati to the Mariners, I got a base hit up the middle against Kansas City. Then Kenny came up and got a base hit to right field. He said he was just trying to hit the ball through the hole because we had a guy on first base. It was good baseball, executed by a good player.

Then when he got to first, I looked at him and he looked at me and we nodded, acknowledging that the first time up, the first time being in a game together, we got base hits. It was very special.

I'm the old pro. I can keep my emotions in check. It took him a little while to do it, but he finally decided he could play, whether his dad was there or not. He decided that he could show his dad (that he could play). But Kenny never really had to show me anything. I always knew what he could do.

Call it genes if you want. But with the genes comes the ability to make the adjustments to hit any pitch at any time — from pitcher to pitcher, pitch to pitch. And that's one of the most important things that he has, along with his concentration level.

Sure, he's always having fun, so everything seems like it comes natural, like he isn't working. But he works very hard. A lot of people don't understand that. Then again, they don't know Kenny like I do. I first saw both the ability to adjust and the concentration level long before Kenny got to the majors. I saw it when he was a kid, about 12 or 13, and I was his batting practice pitcher.

I would never tell him what was coming. I would throw different pitches at him and I could see his concentration level, what he was going to do, how he was going to

approach the ball. I would throw him sliders, curveballs, forkballs, screwballs or change-ups. It didn't matter. He would adjust.

Shortly after that my career took me away from the Reds and Cincinnati, where Kenny, Craig, my wife, Birdie, and I lived. I didn't get to see him play from the time he was 12 until he was 17. I didn't get to see him develop. But Kenny had a good background, growing up around Major League Baseball. Personally, we enjoyed our time together as teammates, and as coach and player, because our relationship is so strong as father and son.

Even when baseball took me away for so many summers, I tried to do as much as possible with him when there was a break in my playing for the Yankees or the Braves. That's where our being such good friends started. So when we got to be teammates, he already understood a lot about what was going on. I explained beforehand that if and when we did become teammates, my presence could take away some of his thunder because it would be so historic and also because I could play. But Kenny understood.

I was there to do something I don't think anybody else will ever get to do again. I told him, "I have never enjoyed playing so much until I got a chance to play with you. So just relax and play the game. Enjoy it, because I am, every minute of it, just playing the game with you."

Claire Smith was a sports columnist for The New York Times in 1996 when she interviewed Ken Griffey Sr. for this story.

Ken Griffey Jr.

chapter 1 stroke of genius

Jay Buhner, Seattle Mariners outfielder
As told to Bob Finnigan

Ken Griffey Jr.'s biggest asset is his confidence. He knows day in, day out, there isn't a thing he can't do on a baseball field and there isn't a pitcher alive he can't hit. Imagine what it's like coming to the park every day knowing that.

You might think Kenny made a big adjustment or some kind of change when he really started to pound homers in 1993, going from 20-27 in previous years to 40 or more. But he didn't change a thing. In fact, over the years his swing hasn't changed at all. Would you tinker with perfection? I wouldn't. I think what happened is he found he could do it and has just kept doing it. Proof he hasn't changed anything is the fact that his batting average has stayed pretty much the same over the years.

The key to his swing is its simplicity. He knows it totally, so the few times something goes wrong, he can fix it quickly. In fact, and this is close to unbelievable, I've seen Ken correct his swing in the same at-bat. Most guys are lucky to do it in a single series or week, and only then after a ton of extra work and film study. Junior's swing is so pure and he knows it so well, he can make instant adjustments after one poor swing.

Technically, his swing is a slight uppercut. In fact, if you look at his Swingman emblem, you can see the bat come around a bit higher than where it starts. He cocks the arm, strides smooth and never lunges. He sort of throws the bat-head at the ball, but he generates such tremendous bat speed that it's tough to see. The arc and torque are perfect.

His swing is so good that he uses the same swing playing golf. It's identical, even though the club is going down to the ground and the ball is stationary. It's still smooth and simple.

Couple that great swing with the fact that he's a smart hitter. He may not have known the league or the pitchers, or even cared, when he started out, but he does

Close observers say Ken's swing didn't change when his home run totals went from the 20s (pre-1992) to the 40s and beyond ('93-present).

now. And he knows the strike zone. He doesn't talk much about it, but he studies pitchers. His focus is great. He has a knack of zoning in on the pitcher's release point. They say that's what makes Tony Gwynn such a great hitter. Well, Junior does it, too.

Picking up the ball out of the pitcher's hand gives a hitter a huge advantage. When time is counted in tenths of seconds, every (instant gained or saved) is immense. When you see the ball sooner, you can adjust to its direction, rotation and speed.

A lot of times we've stood in the on-deck circles before an inning, or when the other team is changing pitchers, and I'll ask Griff,

On May 17, 1998, Griffey hit a three-run homer against Roger Clemens as the Mariners rocked the Rocket for nine earned runs.

"What's this pitcher going to do?" And he'll tell me, "Last time this guy started me off with this, so I'll sit on this or that." Then he goes up there and hits the crap out of the ball. He does that so often you'd swear he had a crystal ball in his hands instead of a bat.

His swing is the source of his power. He's nowhere near as big as other home run hitters. He's gotten bigger over the years and that has helped, but the real key to the distance he gets is bat speed. He is God-gifted strong in his hands and wrists, he gets his trunk mass into every swing and he clears his hips like someone a lot smaller.

Junior rarely gets into a funk. On the rare occasion that he does, he calls home, or his dad will have seen it on ESPN, and he'll call him. Even his mom (Birdie) knows his swing. It's basically his old man's swing with a couple of personal touches. And when he's working on something, few work harder. No one gets to see him work for an hour in early hitting, but he does it a lot,

"There isn't a pitcher alive he can't hit."

in the good times and the bad.

All that ability in a person who has fun doing what he does, a guy who loves to compete and hates to fail, puts Junior in an elite class, both as a competitor and a performer. He is to baseball what Michael Jordan is to basketball. In fact, his excellence has been so consistent that it seems to work against him — not so much with the fans, who consistently vote him tops for the All-Star team each year, but inside the game and especially with the media.

For instance, he ran away with the writers' MVP vote in 1997 but was way down the list in 1998, even though, except for losing 20 points on his batting average (.304-.284), every one of his numbers was virtually the same. So why the big drop-off in the vote? Yeah, the team finished down in the standings, but it was almost as if the media were looking for Junior to do something extra to make them consider him a legit MVP candidate again. That's tough.

Griffey finished '98 with his second straight 56-homer season. He fell 14 short of Mark McGwire's record-shattering total.

Just imagine what his career numbers would be like if he hadn't broken his wrist in 1995. He has a huge metal plate in his wrist and has just one-third flexibility. You see him jam it on a swing at times but he only winces, and he never complains. He just gets in the box for the next pitch. Who knows what his numbers would be without a plate in his wrist? Maybe they'd be one-third higher, instead of 56 homers each of the last two years, maybe 75 homers.

He's a slugger but he tells us all the time he doesn't consider himself a power hitter. He doesn't want the label, because labels are rarely positive things and most are tough to shake. He considers himself a solid five-dimensional player who works every day to get the most out of his ability.

Although they both debuted in the majors at about the same time, Buhner is a full five years older than Griffey.

He takes great pride in what he does. He grew up around the game and was taught to love and respect it by his dad and his dad's friends and teammates. That's why he works at his game. It might not look like it because he makes everything look so easy and so smooth, but he's playing hard and working hard every day.

Close friends off the field, Jay Buhner and Ken Griffey Jr. have formed one of the most lethal home run combinations in baseball history. Before Buhner missed much of the '98 season with an injury, the Mariners' duo combined for 96 homers in 1997, the third-highest home run total behind the 115 Maris/Mantle combination in 1961 and the 107 racked up by Ruth/Gehrig in 1927. Buhner and Griffey combined for 93 round trippers in 1996.

"He is to baseball what Michael Jordan is to basketball."

chapter 2 the natural

Jim Lefebvre, ex-Seattle Mariners manager
As told to John Hickey

The first time I ever saw Ken Griffey Jr. I was coaching third base with Oakland, and Seattle had brought him up at the end of the year. He'd just signed out of high school, and they had him taking batting practice with the team before the game. He wasn't on the big-league roster, but they wanted to see what kind of player they had. I was watching him that first time, and let me tell you, watching him was something. He was just so cool and calm, and it seemed

At Moeller High in Cincinnati, Griffey played baseball and football before becoming the top pick in the '87 baseball draft.

like he belonged there.

There are things you look for the first time you see a guy, especially when a player is so much in the news as he was, being the first pick in the draft and the son of a great player. He wasn't skinny, but he was a little on the thin side, enough so that you couldn't tell how strong he was. But when you saw the ball fly off his bat, you saw something you don't see often — electrifying kind of power. He was a line drive hitter, but you could tell that when he learned to get under the ball, he could clear a few walls in this league. He could really smoke the ball.

In 1989, I was in my first year as the Seattle manager, and during spring training he came up to me while I was leaning against one of the batting cages. I asked him how many spring trainings this was for him. I thought it was one, maybe two. He said, "Nope, this is No. 12 for me." We got to talking, and he started filling me in on all the things he remembered from spring

"He was so natural, and never in awe."

trainings when his dad was with the Reds and later with the Yankees. Here he was a rookie, and he already had a world of experience. What that told me was that he was always around the game. And it showed.

He was so natural, and never in awe. His maturity comes from his exposure to the game with his dad. He always made easy adjustments.

The other thing that made him stand out was that he came to the majors with a lot of enthusiasm. He had fun playing the game, and he injected a lot of enthusiasm into our team. At the time, he was still a teen-ager and, because of his age, he would get along better with the batboys than some of the older guys. He always had great talent and great skills, but he also had this energy and this enthusiasm that people hooked on to right away.

Right from the first, players, and even coaches, gravitated toward him. The manager did, I can guarantee you that. You want

As a 19-year-old at a time when 36 homers was good enough to lead the league, Junior hit .264 with 16 HRs as a rookie.

you see a kid light the world on fire for two or three weeks in the spring, then you mortgage the future to make a spot for him, and then in the final weeks of spring training you see that he's not ready?

You just have to watch his progress, and for Junior, that was never an issue. Junior got better and better. When I made the final decision, I called him into my office and explained all this too him and told him, "Junior, this is the toughest call I've ever had to make." His head was sinking and he got a sad look on his face before I said, "Congratulations. You are my center fielder." He smiled and said, "Thanks, can I call my dad?" I said, "Here's the phone."

Usually it takes three years for a kid to feel he belongs in the majors. For Griffey, that was never the case. From the first day, he was at home in the clubhouse and on the field. The one thing about Junior was that it only took one time. When he had to adjust, he made the corrections right away.

to be around that kind of energy and fire.

That first spring (the decision to bring) him up to the majors went right down to the last day before we broke camp. (General manager) Woody Woodward came to me and said, "It's your call." The one thing I didn't want to do was bring him up and then have to send him down later because he wasn't ready. This kid had never failed, and that was no time to start. How many times do

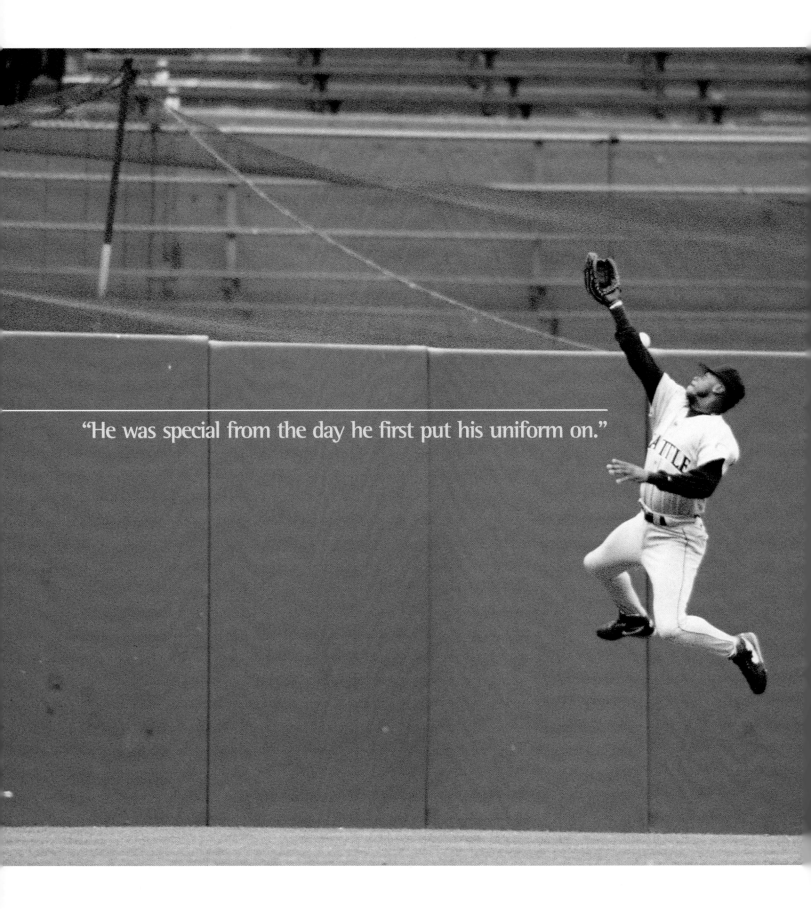

"He was special from the day he first put his uniform on."

The first game, he hit the first pitch he saw from Dave Stewart off the wall.

That was in Oakland. When we got to Seattle for the first time, he hit his first Kingdome pitch for a homer. Imagine that. But we quickly got used to the way Junior rose to the occasion. The guy is an offensive machine. One time we were in the Kingdome and we were having trouble scoring runs. No one was hitting, and in particular, no one was hitting behind him. There were a couple of ways to attack that. One was to move him up in the order. The other was to put the best hitters on the team in front of him, making sure he would hit with lots of men on base. That's what I decided to do.

So I hit him fourth instead of third. He saw the lineup card, and the poor kid was shocked. He came to me, and let me tell you, he was down. He didn't like it, and he said, "I'm not a home run hitter. I'm better off as a second-place hitter." I told him, "Let me make up the lineup."

Griffey impressed early not just with his bat, but also his glove. Catches such as this one soon became routine.

I knew it was just a matter of time before he was a 40-plus home run guy. He didn't think of himself as a home run hitter. Now you look at him and that's all you think about. He was special from the day he first put his uniform on.

There was never a time that I thought we were rushing him to the majors. That doesn't mean there wasn't a chance that we were, but there was just something about him that made it seem unlikely. It was more

In his last year playing for Lefebvre, Griffey hit .327, the highest batting average of his first 10 big-league seasons.

than the great tools he brought to the game on defense or the power in his swing. It was more a matter where here was a guy who was ready like few 19-year-olds ever can be.

He didn't win the Rookie of the Year Award, though, because he was hurt (a broken bone in his right hand) in July, and he wasn't quite the same hitter when he came back. Still, the way he took charge that first year, with his 16 homers and his .264 batting average, it seemed that we were right that he was ready. But, really, nobody could have been wrong betting on this kid.

Jim Lefebvre managed the Mariners in the first three years of the Ken Griffey Jr. era. Seattle improved every year under Lefebvre, including his best year in 1991 when Seattle finished 83-79 behind Griffey's .327 batting average.

chapter 3 Fun and Games

Lee Elia, ex-Seattle Mariners coach
As told to Paul Hagen

I'll never forget the first time I saw Ken Griffey Jr. It was spring training in 1993, and I was on a new staff coming in with Lou Piniella. Without (seeing him) swing a bat or throw a ball, we all felt that it was great to have a franchise player. I think he was only 23 years old at the time, but you could tell, just by his presence, that he was something special.

I never saw anybody who enjoyed playing as much as he did. He didn't put any extra pressure on himself. He WORKED. He worked his own way. If a stranger came down and saw that ballclub for two days, he would have thought Junior presented a laissez-faire approach to things, which really wasn't the case. When he worked, he WORKED.

In the outfield drills, he developed a little bit of leadership: the first one on the field, the first one to do the drill. When he's working he does it with such a sense of fun that you might assume he is fooling around.

And he'll probably always be known as "The Kid" because that's his approach. But he's working all the time. He knows exactly what he's doing. He's extremely prepared.

One time we were playing Oakland and they made a pitching change. On the bench he turned to me and said, "Uncle Lee, who is this guy?" And I said, "I'm not familiar with him either. But this is his name and this is where he's pitched and you may have faced him."

He said, "You know, I DID face him. And he had me 1-and-2 and he came inside on me. He's not going to do that tonight."

As fate could have it only in baseball, the pitcher went 1-2. And he came inside. And Junior hit it into the upper deck.

There are just some attributes the great ones have. It could be because as a kid he hung around his daddy and his daddy was with great ballclubs in Cincinnati. I'm sure that played a part in it.

Even on the back field, even when

"When he's working he does it with a sense of fun."

nobody else is around, he has that great personality. He's bubbly. When he's working and we're alone and he's grinding it out, when he's really getting into the fundamentals of the swing, maybe there are times you feel like he's lazy with his top hand or he's drifting into the pitch. But even then, he does it with a joy. They always say the good ones can work endlessly without getting tired. And that's the way Junior is. When he puts his mind to go the extra mile on a given day, he can stay out there all day and never get tired. Because he's so fluid. And everything is so natural.

In my experience, the guys with great talent usually have a great work ethic. I was never a great player. But in my career (as a manager and coach) I've been very, very blessed. In Philadelphia I was with Mike Schmidt and Pete Rose and Steve Carlton. Then I was with the Yankees and Don Mattingly. Then when I managed the Cubs with Ryne Sandberg and Lee Smith. And

Casual observers might think the always-smiling Griffey doesn't give his all in practice. Coaches and teammates will tell you otherwise.

Seattle where I coached Junior and Randy Johnson and Edgar Martinez and Alex Rodriguez. Somehow I've run into a bunch of Hall of Fame guys. I've been flat-out lucky.

And every one of them has a great understanding of what they can do. And they work at it. They truly do. They start their day at 2 p.m. and they work every day.

In Junior's case, the things he does are so fluid. Like on defense. There were many, many nights in the five years I was with Seattle that a ball would be hit and it would have double written all over it. Then, geez, all of a sudden there's Junior. Offensively, when you would think that everything was stacked against him, somehow he would surface and get the big hit for you.

His leadership is not vocal. He's not one of these guys who's going to stand up in front of the club and say, "We've got to tighten the ship." His leadership is by going out there and enjoying it and playing every day. Very, very few players today go out and give you 160 ball games. But it takes a lot to get Junior out of there. He likes to play.

I think that's because he has a great

In the 1995 AL division playoff series against the Yankees, Griffey hit .391 with five homers in five games.

"The guys with great talent have a great work ethic."

desire to compete and a lot of inner pride. The good ones, when they're asked to deliver, they deliver. He likes that. He likes to be recognized for what he's accomplished, but he doesn't flaunt it. He enjoys it.

When I look at all the other guys over the years who had good natural ability, they may have had to work in some area a little harder. In Junior's case, he's just so natural in everything he does that it's easier for him to enjoy playing. Since he doesn't put pressure on himself, he responds.

Kevin Mitchell had 119 homers from 1989 to '91 but was a disappointment in his one-year stint as Seattle's clean-up hitter behind Griffey.

Sometimes (in Seattle) we used to talk about what it would be like (for Junior) if we were in a big market with a lot more attention. But we found out where he was in '95 when we came back from being 12 games out (to win the AL West). We needed Junior in September, and he — along with a bunch of other guys — was there every night. Then we got into postseason play and the Yankees had us down two games to none, and Junior just led the way. We came back and won the next three. Had the pitching held up, we would have been in the World Series.

I think that was a turning point in his career. Physically, he already had it all. It was just a matter of taking the different parts of his game to the next level.

The biggest change was mental, though. That year (1995) was the first time he's been with a ballclub that had a chance to win, and that was very special to him. Still is. His one real dream would be to someday put a ring on his finger. There was no ques-

tion his MVP year (1997) that he was the Most Valuable Player in the American League. And even the year prior to that he could have won it. Now he's the consummate pro out there. But he still will be Junior. And it's a pleasure to watch him.

I don't think you can compare him to anybody. His makeup. His personality. His tremendous love for kids. If he was in a rush and there were four or five men who wanted to ask him a question or ask for an autograph — and he's always hounded — he might say, "Fellas, I'm busy. I've got to go."

But if you put four or five kids there, he'd make the bus wait.

I don't have the command of the language to really say how special he is. Since he's a superstar, you would expect there might be some things about him you probably wouldn't like. In my five years with the Mariners, I didn't see anything like that.

Lee Elia was the Mariners hitting instructor and bench coach from 1993 to '97. In the first four years of his career without Elia, Griffey hit just 87 home runs. In five years under Elia's tutelage,

Junior amassed 207 homers despite injury-shortened seasons in 1994 and '95.

As Griffey's bat has improved, so has the lineup around him. Edgar Martinez (better than .315 career) and Jay Buhner (averaging 30 HRs per year) provide ample support.

chapter 4 Hit Man

Dave Duncan, St. Louis Cardinals pitching coach
As told to Tom Wheatley

It must have been his first year in the big leagues when I first saw Ken Griffey Jr. play. What I remember is the talk about how talented he was, so I think we all had great expectations of seeing him.

There are certain hitters you feel comfortable going against. You have a pretty good idea how you're going to get them out. You can get them out if you execute pitches. I remember him right away as being somebody requiring special attention. He had some weaknesses. But he was so dangerous every time he walked to the plate that you knew you couldn't make many mistakes without paying for them.

He's really changed. Early on, he was more of a middle-to-the-inside-part-of-the-plate hitter. When I say that, that's where he would hurt you with an extra base hit or a home run. As his skills evolved over the years, he became more of an out-over-the-plate-type hitter, probably because that's where he was pitched so much. By making adjustments to how the pitchers were pitching to him, he became more dangerous out over the plate rather than just inside.

All your good hitters, year to year, make adjustments. If they don't, they're not going to maintain the same level of performance. He did a good job of that. At the same time, he didn't really give up a lot on the inside. He was still able to react on the mistake pitch, so you had to make good pitches if you went inside.

He really improved his discipline in and out of the strike zone. Early on, he would swing at a lot of balls that were above the strike zone. He'd swing at a lot of balls that were below the strike zone. Year to year, he just really shrank his strike zone down. That's what good hitters do. He wasn't satisfied with his performance, and he made the right adjustments.

I'm sure his background had a lot to do with that. During his youth, because of his

Griffey has never had more than 185 hits in a year. The reason: a keen batting eye that results in nearly 70 walks per season.

"He'd give Randy Johnson a good at-bat. He'd give anybody a good at-bat."

father, he was exposed to the major leagues and major league coaching. I'm sure it was ingrained in him that in order to be real good you have to be open-minded. But the swing never changed. It's just a good, solid swing, mechanically sound. He accomplishes all the things you need to accomplish to hit the ball hard, consistently and with power.

He was always pretty tough against left-handers. I never felt that a left-hander had a huge advantage against him, unless it was a special one who threw exceptionally hard and had a real quality breaking ball. If the left-hander could do those things, probably the pitcher had a little advantage. There aren't too many of those pitchers around. He played with Randy Johnson all those years in Seattle, but he would give Randy Johnson a good at-bat. He'd give anybody a good at-bat.

People talk about him (having an advan-

Junior became the seventh youngest player to reach the 1,000-hit plateau with his single off the Twins' Frankie Rodriguez on Aug. 16, 1995.

Griffey, not known for bunting, assumed the position in the '95 playoffs only to be hit by a pitch, setting up Edgar Martinez' grand slam against the Yankees.

tage) hitting in the Kingdome. The year I coached up there, in '82, I thought it would be a real tough park to pitch in. However, over the course of the year, I learned that it was a pretty fair ballpark. If you pulled the ball, it seemed like a small ballpark. But from the power alleys to center field, you've got to hit the ball really well to get it out of there.

But Griffey's capable of hitting the ball out of any part of any ballpark. If he knows he's not going to get anything he can pull, he's capable of hitting the ball to left field out of any ballpark. There aren't many guys who can hit for that kind of an average and with that kind of power. And he's really consistent day in and day out. He's not streaky at all. He might have a period of time where he's not swinging as good as other times, but it never seems like he's struggling.

He's such a well-rounded player, what can he not do? He can play center field with the best of them. He has a good arm. He runs good. He can steal a base. I don't know that I can compare anybody in today's game with him overall. I can't think of anybody. You'd have to talk about guys like Willie Mays and Mickey Mantle and those guys who hit for high averages and a lot of home runs, but I didn't see them play. Griffey's pretty special.

I've never been in the same clubhouse with him, but it seems like he's a good teammate. I say that because you never hear anything but positives about him. About the only thing negative is that some

"He's such a well-rounded player. What can he not do?"

people don't like him wearing his hat backwards during batting practice. In a sense, it's against tradition.

But, you know, to me he looks like he has fun playing the game, and I think that's more important than anything. We don't have enough guys who have fun playing the game and who play hard all the time. I think it sends a very good message to young kids. So as far as I'm concerned, he can do whatever he wants with his hat.

As the pitching coach for Oakland, Dave Duncan had to contend with the bat of Ken Griffey Jr. from his rookie season of 1989 through 1995, after which Duncan joined former A's manager Tony La Russa in St. Louis.

It's not a reach to compare Griffey to Mays and Mantle, two legends on both offense and defense.

chapter 5 the kid

Rickey Henderson, New York Mets outfielder
As told to John Hickey

Ken had to be about 14, maybe 15, when I first met him. To me, he was always a great kid, and it didn't take long to see that he was going to be a great athlete, too.

He enjoyed playing sports, and not just baseball, either. I was young myself at the time (1985, when he joined the Yankees), and so I saw him as someone who had always loved to go out and play the game. And I took the time to go out with him and play. I had always looked up to his father, and now we were on the same team, and I had more free time than his father.

If you go out next to the players' parking lot at Yankee Stadium, there are a couple of baseball fields and some basketball courts. Sometimes he and I would play catch after a game, but other times we'd go across the street and play basketball after games.

And it wouldn't stop there. During spring training we lived in the same apartment complex, and when I played in New York, we

All-time stolen base leader Rickey Henderson played with Ken Griffey Sr. in New York in 1985 and '86.

lived in the same complex in New Jersey. So we were always around each other. Anytime we had a chance to throw a ball or shoot a ball, we did.

We liked to do a lot of things together. I love to fish, and he and his father and I would throw our poles in the ponds around the complex we stayed in. It was just him and his father and me, and even then, he was so competitive. As a little kid, it was so amazing to see that he was as competitive as he was about wanting to win. Sometimes when you see that in a kid — that no matter what happens he's going to get back up and battle — that means he's at least going to be a competitor. When you look at him today, you can still see that fierce competitive drive.

He was a killer basketball player, but he didn't have all the moves quite then. I used

The Griffeys scored back-to-back runs in this father-son game. The duo later hit big-league back-to-back homers with Seattle.

"As a kid, it was amazing to see that he was as competitive as he was."

to beat him all the time. I think what he would probably remember more — and it's something I certainly remember more — was the last time we were out on the playground playing "horse." It had been a hard day, and I was tired, so I said I'd play a game or two more.

So we played the first game, and I ended up winning it. Then, toward the end of the second game, I was getting tired. I was at the last letter, where if he missed and I hit, it's over. So he misses, and the ball bounces all the way across the court, over by where my car is. I get the ball, shoot it and the ball hits nothing but the bottom of the net. Then I jump in my car, and I'm leaving.

That's it. And he comes running after my car. He yells, "I don't care what happens, I'm going to play you until I die. I'm going to beat you before I die." But I never played him again.

When I think back on all that time he spent around the clubhouse, what came out

Shagging fly balls in the outfield with Dad at spring training helped Junior develop the talent that would make him a superstar.

of it was that it made him appreciate the game. It made him know what it takes to be a professional ballplayer and what it takes to be a success. He had a good father and mother. They taught him well. He learned the game from his father, who was a great player.

To me, with kids who have parents who played the game, sometimes they don't really like the game and you have to force them to play it. Not with Ken. It so happened that he enjoyed the game as much as his father did. Ken always looked up to his father. He wanted to be just like him.

The first time I knew he was going to be something special as a player was the second year I was with the Yankees (1986). I came to spring training that year and he'd grown about six inches. The year before, he'd been about chest-high to me, and all of a sudden he was taller than me. I couldn't believe over the winter that he had grown that much. When we went out to play that

spring, he was catching the ball with no problem and running around the field like he knew what he was doing. That's when I knew he was going to be a good player.

But he was always a good athlete. I think when he was a little kid his father put a ball in his hand, and he's been an athlete ever since. I think he looked up to me because of the type of player I was, but I think he respected me more as a person because I was his friend and as a kid he could go out and play with me. He enjoyed that time,

Ken Griffey Sr. actually has two sons who played professional baseball: Craig (left) and Ken Jr.

and I know I sure did, too. I take only a little credit for the player he is, though. I tried to teach him that the game was fun and you could have a lot of fun in it, but the main influence on Ken was his parents. They taught him right, and his father made him the player he is today.

His father was a great influence on me, and I know he had to be a great influence on Ken, too. I loved the way his father played the game, the way he carried himself and his dedication. I know it rubbed off on Ken as much as it did on me. There were some little things I helped him out with, such as playing in the outfield and running the bases, but he was more in awe and happy that I took the time to go out and play with him.

We are still in touch and have always been pretty close. In the off-season, I will probably talk to him three or four times, and usually I'll see him in Hawaii. When I do, he's still always looking for that chance

As a kid, Griffey was quite the stolen base threat himself. He swiped 32 in just 58 games for minor league San Bernardino in '88.

to get me back on the basketball court. He still wants to beat me. It's that competitive thing, I guess. He wants that chance to get even.

One day, maybe I'll give him that chance again. I never gave him the chance after that last time, and he still talks about it.

Rickey Henderson, baseball's all-time stolen base king, broke into the big leagues in 1979 and has played with six different teams: Oakland, N.Y. Yankees, Toronto, San Diego, Anaheim and, most recently, the N.Y. Mets. He became friends with the Griffeys during his stint with the Yankees from 1985 to '89.

chapter 6 wish upon a star

Cindy Hoppner, Wish Director, Make-A-Wish
Foundation of Washington State
As told to Aaron Derr

"The amazing thing is the amount of time he spends with the children."

Ken Griffey Jr. has played in Seattle since 1989. He was such a big deal when he first came to Seattle, and he's an even bigger deal today. Jayson was the first child to wish to meet Ken Griffey Jr. Jayson was an adorable 5-year-old with a heart defect. He wore a tiny little suit and a gold bow tie to his meeting with Griffey at a game in 1989.

After the game, Jayson and his family were scheduled to go to the Space Needle for dinner. Jayson spontaneously asked Griffey if he wanted to come along, and Griffey said yes. During dinner, Griffey got up and went home to get one of his own jerseys for the child. When they were riding back to the hotel in the limousine, Jayson fell asleep in Griffey's arms. Griffey still talks about that wish in interviews today. He says he'll never forget his first wish.

We granted a wish on the last game of the Mariners' 1998 season for Marshall, a 7-year-old boy from Spokane, Wash. Marshall takes baseball very seriously, and he wished for the experience of throwing out a pitch in a major league ballpark in front of a big crowd. I had asked Ken Griffey Jr. to catch Marshall's pitch, and Griffey said he'd do it, but after he went into the clubhouse and met Marshall, Griffey came out and said to me, "Here's the deal. He doesn't WANT me to catch the pitch because I'm not a catcher. He wants Dan Wilson to catch."

That's how serious Marshall was about the whole thing. Thing is, Dan Wilson (Seattle's starting catcher) wasn't scheduled to play that day. So Griffey said, "I've got it all worked out. I'm gonna get Dan to suit up in full catcher's gear, and (Texas Rangers outfielder) Juan Gonzalez is going to hit."

So Dan suited up and caught the pitch, with Gonzalez at-bat, and Marshall threw a fantastic pitch from the mound. Marshall wasn't too happy about it at first. When he came off the field, Marshall said to Griffey and Alex Rodriguez and David Segui, "I

Many Mariners players have given their time to Make-A-Wish, but no one lights up a kid's face like Ken Griffey Jr.

tried my best." And Griffey, Segui and Rodriguez all said, "You did great. It was a low fastball. He can't hit the low fastball. There's no way he can hit that pitch!"

Marshall met the entire team, and all of the big team mascots (since it was Mascot Day and all), and later said that was the best day of his life.

Griffey has met 31 kids since 1989 just through Make-A-Wish, and every single one of those wishes is just as fabulous. The most amazing thing is the amount of time he spends with the children. Typically, a wish visit with him will last between 1-1/2 and two hours. That's a lot of time for what we call a "celebrity wish."

Sometimes he's taking batting practice during that time, but he certainly does not appear to be that serious about batting practice. And he doesn't seem to like to stretch, but sometimes he'll stretch with the Wish child. He just hangs out with the kid, takes him into the clubhouse and shows him his

Children aren't the only ones who want to meet Ken Griffey Jr., but the Kid seems to prefer the company of younger fans.

locker. They normally don't let women back there, but they made an exception for the one girl who wished to meet him. They cleared out the locker room and he went back there with her.

One time he flew from Florida to Seattle during the off-season to meet a child in the hospital. He had no other reason to come to Seattle other than to see that child.

Each wish he grants is tailored specifically to the child. Just this past season, he met a boy who came from very limited means and was very, very shy. He wouldn't speak for the first hour. He brought nothing with him for Ken to sign, so the child's dad went and bought two packs of cards and a couple of balls for the team members to sign. So Ken sent a ballboy around the clubhouse with the two balls and all the cards. No one asked him to do that, he just took it upon himself to make it happen. A little while later he presented the boy with baseball cards individually signed by each player, and two base-

balls signed by every player on the team.

At the end of the wish, Griffey finally had this kid laughing about how Jay Buhner was going to shave his head. They had the kid set up and ready to have his head shaved, and the kid was just cracking up, but then they couldn't find the shears. So by the end of the visit this kid, after not talking for an hour, was laughing and ready to have his head shaved by Jay Buhner.

Griffey can talk anybody into anything. Not because he intimidates people, but because he's a charmer.

I think Ken Griffey Jr. is a kid himself. He loves kids and is so good with them. He is such an easy-going, comfortable person, he puts the kids at ease. Every time I see a child meet him, the coolest thing is to see the look on their faces when they see him for the first time. They are usually quite talkative and animated until Griffey comes out of the clubhouse for the first time, and then they clam up. They just freeze, because . . . there he is.

Give him 10 minutes, and Griffey can turn even the shiest child into quite the conversationalist.

Right in front of them. But I'd say within 15 to 20 minutes, Griffey has them just laughing and talking and just totally relaxed. He just relates really well to kids.

I think he's been very, very moved by some of his experiences with Wish kids. Wish kids are different in some ways. They're still kids, but also, they've gone through a lot, and they have somewhat of a different perspective on life. I think Ken's picked up on that and has really seen the power of a wish. He loves to give, he is a great role model, he works hard and, of course, he is a great player. Every child who wishes to meet him says he's the greatest player in baseball. They are in such awe of him.

He met another boy in 1998, a 6-year-old with a brain tumor that affected his eyesight. His vision was very poor, but he wanted to play catch with Ken Griffey Jr. I thought, "Well, maybe he'll spend a couple of minutes out there with him." He and that kid played catch for at least 20 minutes. The boy caught, I think, two balls the entire time, and he spent the rest of the time chasing after the ball. The kid had front-row seats, and Griffey hit two home runs that night and dedicated both of them to the Wish child he had played catch with just a few hours before.

Cindy Hoppner has been with the Seattle-based Make-A-Wish Foundation of Washington State, one of 81 Make-A-Wish chapters across the United States, since 1996. The organization grants Wishes to children between 2-1/2 and 18 years of age with life-threatening illnesses. Referrals to the Make-A-Wish Foundation of America can be made at 1-800-722-9474.

Griffey often requests background info from Make-A-Wish so he can tailor the experience specifically for the child.

chapter 7 sudden impact

Tony La Russa, St. Louis Cardinals manager
As told to John Hickey

Obviously, when Ken Griffey Jr. got to the major leagues with Seattle, he was so young with so little experience. As the opposing manager, your first impression had to be, "Hey, we can exploit him a little, or we can exploit him a lot."

But it was very apparent from the first look at him that this guy was special. Right from that first game, he was already good by big-league standards. The idea we had was to get this guy now, get him before he realized just how good he was, but we found out quickly that there was no grace period.

We had the Mariners on Opening Day in the Coliseum. Typically, when you have a young hitter you have never faced before, there are standard things you can do to him. You know, you can set him up with breaking pitches, or test him with fastballs. You don't know if a young guy like that has a weakness, but if he does, you want to take advantage of that inexperience.

Right away he sent a real strong message that, "I'm not a normal guy," by ripping a ball off the wall in his first at-bat against Dave Stewart. You have to remember that at the time, Stew had a style he would go to, an aura, and he made a habit of making things miserable for kids like that. But he didn't make many problems for Mr. Griffey. And we saw later that year that not many other pitchers made problems for him. He's turned into one of the

Although Griffey played just 129 games in the minors, he's never been intimidated by even the best pitchers, Dave Stewart included.

"With Griffey, he started good, and he became great."

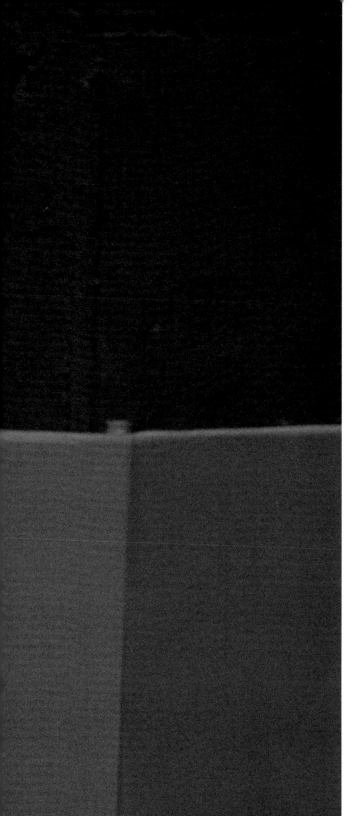

great offensive forces in the game.

As a manager, you are always looking for ways your team, particularly your pitchers, can adapt to a star like that. With Griffey, he started good, and he became great. When you start good, there aren't huge improvements that a player makes, so there aren't great adaptations you can make to defend against him. The one thing you can really see as he has played for a number of years now is that he's gotten more leverage in his swing and gotten more lift on the ball. He came to the majors with a classic line drive swing. Now that classic line drive has become a classic bomb.

You always think about how to deal with his power potential. But if you focus too much on that, you forget about the rest of his game. The impact he has defensively is a powerful force. He's had that kind of impact from the very beginning. It's not talked about much, but he beats you just in the way he cuts balls off in the alleys

The Kid instantly caught on in the field, as well. In just his second big-league season, he snared his first Gold Glove.

and by the way he gets to balls in the air that other center fielders just wouldn't get to. And he gets his glove over the fence as well as anyone. On top of that, he has an innate sense of timing his throws, so it makes him exceptionally difficult to run against. Let's face it: He's the complete package on defense.

It hasn't hurt him any that he's played in a lineup like Seattle's with Edgar Martinez and Jay Buhner and, in the last couple of years, Alex Rodriguez. But he's probably more important to their hitting

than they are to his. In team meetings before facing the Mariners, you have to spend as much time thinking about getting Edgar out as you do thinking about getting Junior out. But Griffey's the RBI machine for them. The thing is, you can take one hitter out of any lineup by the way you pitch to him or the way you avoid pitching to him. But in Seattle, even if you walk Junior, all that does is put one more guy on base for the other really good hitters. As a manager, there are times you have to walk him, but because of that strong line-up, there are fewer times than you would think.

As long as he's in the lineup, he creates better at-bats for the other guys, and his impact on the lineup can't be overrated. Alex can hit no matter where he bats and no matter who bats behind him, but I'll flat-out guarantee you that he is a better hitter because he hits in front of Ken Griffey.

Griffey was a fixture at the All-Star Game well before his hard-hitting teammates earned their just due.

One of the things that is the most telling about Griffey is the overall excellence of his play every day. For every game where you see him make a great play or get the game-winning hit, it seems like there are dozens of other games where he's done exactly the same things. And if you are on the other side, as I was so much of the time, that's unfortunate. But he brings all those different abilities he has to the game every day.

The only part of his game that has fallen off a little is that he used to be more of a steal threat. But Lou Piniella knows what he's doing. Lou's careful with him. And they've got to be cautious. You don't want a player like that to come up with some kind of leg problem just because he slid into second base wrong on a steal.

To me, it seems probably the most difficult part of his career would have been his rookie year. You have to give Jim Lefebvre a lot of credit. Jim had been a coach for

Although he was a consistent stolen base threat during his minor league career, Griffey's highest steals total in the majors is 20.

me, and he got to Seattle at the same time that Junior was about ready to break through. And for Jim, it was a tough call whether or not to bring him to the major leagues as a teen-ager or to wait.

Everybody knew Jim had a can't-miss player on his hands. But those guys do miss sometimes. And the way those guys miss is because they aren't handled properly with their first exposure to the big leagues. Jim and I talked about it at the time, and I know Jim was reluctant to bring Junior to the majors that early in his career.

But that first spring, Griffey was just so outstanding. He impressed us every time we saw him. What Jim was facing was one of the toughest calls a manager can make, because you are talking about possibly one of the great careers in the game. If Junior fails in that first shot and has to get sent back to the minors, you as the manager are going to hear about it for a long time. It was a great evaluation on Jim's part,

because he saw that the maturity and the game-readiness Griffey had then was enough for him to be turned loose in the majors.

The thing is, anyone could have said, "In three years, this kid is going to be our center fielder and one of the best in the game." Jim didn't have that call to make. He said, "He's our center fielder right now," and that was a pretty good call, I think you'd have to say.

Few people are better qualified to assess Ken Griffey Jr. than Tony La Russa, who was Oakland's manager from 1986 to 1995 before leaving for St. Louis. Under La Russa, the A's won four AL West titles and appeared in three World Series.

As Oakland's manager, even Tony La Russa had to admire Griffey's breakout season of 1993: .309, 109 RBI and 45 homers.

"Now that classic line drive has become a classic bomb."

chapter 8 the gold standard

Bobby Murcer, ex-Yankees center fielder
As told to Pat McEvoy

"The one thing Junior does is he challenges those walls out there."

If you're looking for a complete player in center field, I think Ken Griffey Jr. pretty much fills all the qualifications. He's got speed. He has a good arm. He has great instincts. He's a man who will quarterback the outfield, which a center fielder should do. Plus, he's earned respect. One of the things I respect is the fact that he's played alongside more than 20 different left fielders in Seattle.

He's been able to adjust (to his different outfielders). One of the things that makes a center fielder a better center fielder is knowing (the strengths and weaknesses) of the players in left field and right field. Griffey has great instincts that allow him to adjust to them. He's able to be the quarterback out there and to make sure they don't have any collisions and that they know their limitations.

Basically, I think the biggest assets a center fielder could have are speed and

quickness. Obviously, the center fielder plays in the most spacious part of the ballpark. So it's easier to see the angle of the baseball when it goes into the air, and if you've got the speed, you can run down a lot of fly balls. One of the things that speed and instinctive quickness allow you to do is to get the jump on the ball so you can play more shallow in center and still run down the ball if it's hit over your head. I would say maybe more than 60 percent of the base hits drop in front of you in center field and not over your head. Maybe even 70 percent.

The keys are knowing the pitcher, know-

Just two other outfielders come close to Griffey's nine straight Gold Gloves. Al Kaline and Paul Blair each had seven straight.

ing the location of the pitch — you can see the location by seeing if the catcher is moving inside or outside — and knowing who the hitter is — whether he's a guy who has some power or whether he hits the ball to the opposite field. If you can compute all that in your mind, you have a better chance of catching it.

Griffey's made so many great catches I don't think I can pick one that stands out in my mind. The one thing Junior does is he challenges those walls out there. Just having that great ability to be able to time the ball, to be able to get back there and leap and keep his eye on it, is amazing. He does it all the time. He's made some great catches at Yankee Stadium climbing the wall and going above the wall to bring back home runs.

The hardest place to play in Yankee Stadium, especially the old Yankee Stadium, may actually be left field because it's very difficult to find the right depth to play. You always found yourself playing too deep out

To cover all that ground in center field, you have to have speed, and without question, Griffey's got some to burn.

The Mariners may go through left fielders like crazy, but Griffey and Buhner have starred together as center and right fielder since 1991.

To be a good center fielder, first and foremost, you have to have speed. That's the No. 1 ingredient in my opinion. Second of all, you must have the great instincts to utilize that speed: to be able to get the jump on the ball, to anticipate where it is going to be and to get your fanny over there in a hurry.

Having a good arm, that's also important in center field, as well as being able to position yourself. I think you have to have a better arm to play right field, but I don't think you need as much speed in right field as you do in center. The guys playing today, your top-notch center fielders, have exceptional speed.

Griffey has all those tools. When he was just a little boy, he and all of our kids, including my son, used to play underneath Yankee Stadium around where the locker rooms were. Junior was such a (great) athlete that you could be standing with him in the hallway and the next thing you knew he'd just do a back flip. He had all kinds of

there because there was so much space. A lot of outfielders would guide themselves by how far away they were from the fence.

Griffey doesn't have to play in some of the toughest places. Candlestick Park (now called 3Com Park) also has to be one of the toughest places in the world to play the outfield because of the way the wind swirls. The Astrodome is very difficult, too, the biggest complaint being you can't see the ball when it goes into the air. The Metrodome has a similar effect, as well, in that you can lose the ball in the roof.

As if his nimble feet weren't enough, Griffey has a strong enough arm to cut down unsuspecting baserunners.

"To be a good center fielder, first and foremost, you have to have speed."

talents and abilities — the agility just to be standing there talking to you and suddenly do a back flip. My son used to say, "You can't believe what Junior is doing down there." At the time, Griffey was probably 11 or 12 years old.

I have some great memories of baseball, knowing that those kids were down there playing while we were playing the games. I mean, they would ride with us to the ballpark, and they couldn't wait to get there so they could form their own game in the tunnels of Yankee Stadium while we played on the field. They never did see one inning of our games, except maybe when they'd take a break in the locker room, where they would watch a pitch or two when the television set would be on. But they couldn't wait to get back out there and start playing. They would take an old sanitary sock, roll it up into a ball and put tape on it, and that was their baseball. After the game, they'd ask, "Who won the game? How'd you do, Dad?"

No question, Junior has exceptional talent, he has exceptional instincts and the abilities to do a lot of things other people can't do.

Bobby Murcer, who spent 13 years of his 17-year career with the Yankees, won a Gold Glove in 1972 and was known as one of the better defensive center fielders in the game. He played with Ken Griffey Sr. in New York in 1982 before joining the Yankees' broadcast booth in 1983. He still serves as the Yankees' TV color commentator for MSG and WPIX broadcasts.

From 1989 to 1997, Ken Griffey Jr. earned more than 23 million combined All-Star votes.

chapter 9 great expectations

Reggie Jackson, Hall of Fame power hitter
As told to John Hickey

The first time most people saw Ken Griffey Jr. was when he was 18 years old and already in the big leagues (in his rookie season in 1989). He was pretty much already a polished player. Everybody saw that. It didn't take any special skill on my part or on anybody else's part to recognize a super talent like his. When he came up, he already had most of the skills you'd want a player to have.

For Junior, he came up in a similar situation to the one I had when I came up with Kansas City and then with Oakland (in 1967 and '68). He came up with a club that was not that good of a team at that time. (Seattle was 73-89, 26 games behind the first-place A's, in 1989.) The Oakland and Kansas City A's back when I broke in were not that good, either. (The A's went 62-99 in 1967 and 82-80 in 1968.) That meant he had one heck of an opportunity to make his mark, and he took advantage of it.

What makes him so good is simple: He's got more talent than most other players. He might have more talent than anybody other than maybe Barry Bonds and a few other players. I mean, Bernie Williams and some of those other guys are terrific players, but I don't think any of them are in Griffey's class.

A lot of the time, people just don't realize how good Junior is. Here is a guy who

Baseball analysts are beginning to anoint Griffey with the title once held by Barry Bonds: baseball's best all-around player.

"A lot of the time, people just don't realize how good Junior is."

Lost in all the hype of Mark McGwire's monstrous 1998 season was another terrific year from Griffey: 56 home runs and 146 RBI.

has hit 56 homers two years in a row (in 1997 and '98), and no one talks about him. No one writes all that much about him.

Mark McGwire is similar to Junior in that respect. Look at the 1998 season. Sammy Sosa hits 66 homers and it's a big deal, a huge deal. McGwire hits 70, and yet by the end of the season he doesn't get any more ink than Sammy. A guy like a McGwire or a Griffey has such high expectations put on him that they practically need to hit at least 10 home runs more than the next guy to really shake things up and make people take notice. That's the way it is with Junior. He hits 56, and people say he could have done better.

I think that's why sometimes you'll see Junior get surly. Those kinds of expectations are unrealistic and hard to live with. It's not that people don't think Junior's a great player. They do. But while they appreciate his greatness as a player, they don't always know how to express it.

At this stage of his career, with all he's done and all he can do, I think if you are starting a team from scratch, you either have to make Griffey your first pick or you have to take his shortstop (Alex Rodriguez, who compiled a .313 average to go along with 101 homers in his first three full big-league seasons). Take either one of those two guys, and you can't go wrong.

"Here is a guy who hit 56 homers two years in a row and no one talks about him."

When I look at Junior's swing, I don't think it's at all like mine. I'm 6-foot; Junior is like 6-3, maybe a little taller. On top of that, he's a lot more lanky than I was at his age. When he swings, his height helps give him a lot more leverage through the strike zone. Overall, Junior has a smoother swing. When his swing is on, it seems like it takes less effort than mine did. He's so smooth that way. It's a natural swing.

The extra element in his game is his background, the fact that he grew up in baseball. When you have that kind of background it allows you to relax and not be that excited when you get to the major leagues. When you get there it's just like going home. You grew up there, so why should you ever be uncomfortable? There's no way you will ever be overwhelmed with the major league facility. It's been a huge advantage to Junior, to Bonds and to many others who had fathers who played in the major leagues.

Reggie Jackson knows a thing or two about home runs. The two-time World Series MVP, nicknamed Mr. October because of his penchant for coming up big in the postseason, hit 563 round trippers during his 21 seasons in the big leagues. Early in his career, Jackson had a similar impact as Ken Griffey Jr., hitting 29 home runs as a rookie before breaking out for 47 homers and 118 RBI in his sophomore season. However, Jackson has what Griffey wants: a World Series ring (five of them, actually). Jackson led the A's to world titles in 1972, '73 and '74 and helped the Yankees win it all in 1977 and '78.

Reggie Jackson and Ken Griffey Jr. both began their careers with teams that were struggling at the time. Jackson went on to win five World Series.

chapter 10 second to none

Tim McCarver, FOX broadcaster
As told to Marty Noble

"There haven't been many players who can take over a game like he can."

I would say Ken Griffey Jr. is the best player in the game today. He is the whole package. In the early or mid-'90s, I might have said Barry Bonds was the best player. But not anymore.

There haven't been many players who can take over a game like he can. It's not very common that a player other than a pitcher can take over a game in baseball. You've got to have opportunity. You can't make your own opportunities in baseball. Pitchers have the opportunity just by the nature of their position. Some hitters can win a game with two or three big hits, but I'm not sure that qualifies as "taking over a game."

Usually a player has to wait for his opportunity. The best center fielder in the game can't do a thing if the ball's never hit to center field.

But having said that, Junior has as much of a chance to dominate a game as anyone. He can hit two home runs and a single, steal a base, throw out a runner and make two brilliant catches in the same game and no one would come away surprised that he did all that. They'd be impressed, but not surprised. He has so many skills that he can get more opportunities than another player in the same position. I mean, what doesn't he do?

But there's also more to it. There's the joy he gets out of performing. In that way, he's like Michael Jordan. You know he appreciates playing. He still likes to make the plays we all wanted to make when we were kids. He plays like a "junior."

In a sense, Griffey is the Jordan of baseball, I think, in that he is recognized within his sport as the No. 1 player. But Junior doesn't have the international status Michael has, nor has his team won or dominated the league as Michael's team has.

In addition, I think there are maybe eight or nine cities — L.A., Chicago, Atlanta and the Northeast corridor — where, if

In Griffey's breakout season of 1993, he tied a major league record by hitting home runs in eight straight games.

Griffey played in any one of them, he'd have twice the name recognition. It's not just that Seattle is a smaller city, but it's more isolated than any team in sports except Edmonton in hockey.

If you're in Philadelphia and you want to see the Yankees, it's two hours by car. You can drive to Baltimore. It's a short flight to Boston. Fans in San Francisco might want to see Junior play, but it's a long trip to see him unless the Mariners are in Oakland.

That said, my sense of it is that he remains the most recognizable name in baseball. When we started (broadcasting baseball) at FOX, our research showed that he was the most recognizable name by a

Before he turned 28, Griffey had 294 homers, 14 more than Mickey Mantle had at the same age. Mantle ranks eighth all-time with 536 dingers.

landslide over Cal Ripken Jr., two or three times more recognized than anyone else in the game. Now that may have changed with Sammy Sosa and Mark McGwire hitting all the home runs and with the Yankees winning again. But it hasn't changed that much.

And it's different with Junior. He's "Junior." The name is part of the image. Cal Ripken Jr. is a "junior," too. And he set the consecutive games played record. But THE junior is Junior, Ken Griffey Jr.

They were both a part of healing the game (after the 1994-95 work stoppage). They were a salve for the game. Cal had to set the record to be a part of it. He broke the unbreakable record. But Junior just had to play. He just had to show up at the park and play. People feel good when they see him play. He's a bright guy with bright eyes. He has major star power. If I were a kid I would want to see him play.

I'm an adult and I still enjoy him.

The name helps, too. Certain names fit better than others. You know what Harry Caray used to say? "Rod Carew. With a name like Rod Carew, how can you not hit?" I agreed. It's all part of the image that has come together for Junior. The smile, the name, the skills.

You don't hear much about him that isn't positive. There's a lot of respect for him in the game. He doesn't complain about

money. He just plays for his contract. People respect that. He's an ambassador for the game without really trying to be.

I got to see Willie Mays play when I was a rookie. I watched him closely. The only other player who was like that for me, for a while, was Fred Lynn in '75 when I was with the Red Sox. You felt obliged to watch him. If I could concentrate on one player now, Griffey would be one of them. I can't say I wouldn't want to watch Nomar Garciaparra or Greg Maddux or McGwire if they were on the same field. And if I was watching Junior, I'd miss Alex Rodriguez. But you have to watch Junior.

Baseball players aren't always great athletes. Some can't run. I think that would be the most common weakness. But you can play the game without speed. A lot of us have proved that over the years. Sometimes you find players with speed who don't have strength or power. But what is it that Junior doesn't have or do well? Like I said,

"If I were a kid I would want to see him play."

it's the complete package, fully loaded.

Willie was a great athlete — speed, strength, soft hands, hand-to-eye coordination, instinct. Mickey Mantle had awesome power and speed and hand-to-eye coordination. He was a great athlete. Frank Robinson was right there. And Henry Aaron . . . if he hadn't been on a mission to break the home run record, he would have shown how great an athlete he was. He was a much better player in the '50s and early '60s than later on when he was trying to pull everything. When I first saw Henry, there wasn't any part of the game that he didn't excel in.

All those guys, they had great athletic skills. And the great ones usually have skills that translate to other sports. Junior doesn't have NBA size, but he can play basketball. And I think he could be a Shannon Sharpe-type in football, a good wide receiver. He could beat Deion Sanders.

Junior has everything a player can have, and he consistently shows that. He has all

the weapons, and his weapons are so good that any one of them can beat you on a given day. When he gets two or three of them into the act, then you've got one of those special games where he just takes over.

Tim McCarver, a big-league catcher for 21 seasons (1959 to 1980), is one of just seven modern-day players to perform in four decades. He has been announcing games for the New York Mets since 1983, and he also analyzes national games for the FOX network.

Regarded by many as the best baseball analyst working today, McCarver knows true greatness when he sees it.

Photography by Tom DiPace/Tom DiPace Photography

Front cover photo by Michael O'Neill/Outline

Additional photography by
    Allsport USA
    Mel Bailey
    Jeff Carlick/Sports Photo Masters
    Cincinnati Reds
    Rich Clarkson/Allsport USA
    Tomasso Derosa/Allsport USA
    Stephen Dunn/Allsport USA
    Otto Greule/Allsport USA
    Major League Baseball
    Make-A-Wish Foundation of Washington State
    National Baseball Hall of Fame
    Outline
    Photo File/TV Sports Mailbag
    Janice E. Rettalita/Allsport USA
    Damian Strohmeyer/Allsport USA
    Ron Vesely/Ron Vesely Photography

Writers

Aaron Derr, who interviewed Cindy Hoppner,
    is an associate editor for Beckett Publications.
Bob Finnigan, who interviewed Jay Buhner,
    covers the Mariners for the *Seattle Times*.
John Hickey, who interviewed Rickey Henderson,
    Reggie Jackson, Tony La Russa and Jim Lefebvre,
    is a sportswriter for the *Oakland Tribune*.
Paul Hagen, who interviewed Lee Elia,
    covers the Phillies for the *Philadelphia Daily News*.
Marty Noble, who interviewed Tim McCarver,
    covers the New York Mets for *Newsday*.
Pat McEvoy, who interviewed Bobby Murcer,
    covers the New York Yankees for *Yankees Magazine*.
Tom Wheatley, who interviewed Dave Duncan, is a sports
    columnist and feature writer for the *St. Louis Post Dispatch*.